THE BEGINNER'S GUIDE TO BLOGGING

25 ESSENTIAL TIPS FOR TURNING YOUR BLOGGING PASSION INTO PROFIT

DAVID GRETE

Visit David Grete at his Advise Author Publishing author page.

This book is dedicated to my family and friends. The happiness I have found in life has come from knowing and being a part of their lives and for that I'm very thankful.

CONTENTS

PREFACE

I've written this guide with a singular goal in mind. I wanted to give my readers the practical and actionable advice to become a successful blogger.

There are several other books out there that instruct on the exciting world of blogging but that being said, I still felt that there was a lot to be desired in books on this topic.

Within this book you can find the practical information and advice needed to create a fantastic blog which is both inspirational and profitable.

No longer shall we be bound to work the typical hours required of a full-fledged member of the rat race. No longer shall we be forced to sell our time as a wage slave to a company that wouldn't think twice about letting us go if it made sense to their bottom line.

Congratulations for taking a chance and beginning on this journey with me. I hope you find a wealth of actionable ideas here that can be useful in your future endeavors as a professional blogger.

Sincerely,

David Grete

CHAPTER 1 : AN INTRODUCTION TO BLOGGING

*I*t all started about a decade ago when the economy went south and I lost my job. I found myself without purpose, surviving on unemployment checks and aimlessly searching for an alternative way to earn a living. Contrarily, losing my job was one of the best things that has ever happened to me.

I didn't even like the job as it involved the despicable act of calling people during dinner. Yes, you guessed it, I was a telemarketer.

Suffice to say instead of feeling disappointment

and despair at the thought of being released and collecting unemployment benefits, I accepted my new predicament as best I could.

The part I didn't handle so well was the uncertainty. How was I going to support myself? What was I going to do with myself? Every day I faced the daunting task of finding a new job, no easy feat during the great financial crash of 2008-2009 and the biggest economic downturn in my life.

One thing I was certain about was that whatever I did, above all, I needed a change. Working in an office completing mundane tasks for a faceless corporation wasn't me. It had some benefits but I was literally going nowhere, like a hamster in its wheel.

I knew I had to resist the temptation of a safe pay check. Resist the temptation to accept my place as a wage slave of the modern world. And resist the temptation of jumping back on my wheel and living the hamster life again.

Time, the most valuable asset of all, provided me with a rare opportunity that few experience in their career driven lives. It gave me time to think and plan. Who do I want to be? What do I want to do with my life?

I decided I wanted to be free of the bonds and shackles of the nine-to-five office cubicle. The only way I would work that hard again would be if I worked for myself.

So, without a clear direction, I spent hours searching for ways to start my new business. I didn't have much start-up capital to invest, so I needed something with a low entry barrier. What I found was mostly scams and get rich quick schemes.

I'd heard of the possibilities of blogging. There were a few bloggers doing what I could only dream of doing. I gave it some consideration and contacted some of them. Some were kind enough to answer my emails and some gave me some solid advice on getting started in the blogging game.

They all appeared to be quite successful with their blogs. They wrote about things they enjoyed and were all passionate about connecting with their readers.

I quickly realized, the formula for a successful blog was sitting there in front of me. So, I got my notebook out and began putting together my ideas for my blog, and before long I launched my very first blog.

It's taken me several years complete this first

edition. Much of it was written several years ago while I was struggling to make a living. But the book takes you through my entire experience from those struggles to the success in recent years.

The success I found in sharing what I had learned about blogging and making a living online was significant. From my experience alone I've proven that it is possible to make a lot of money from blogging and if you've got the right attitude, you too can achieve your goals.

I designed my most successful blog to teach people about making money online through online marketing and search engine optimization (SEO).

I researched and wrote about interesting and practical topics to further build my readership. I picked up a few pointers given on how to grow web traffic and successfully monetize it.

It was at this point that I learned about Pareto's Principle. This is commonly known as the "80-20 Rule" and it states that on average only 20 percent of your actions generate 80 percent of your results (high value).

However, the remaining 80 percent of your actions only generate 20 percent of your results (low value). So, if this is true, I thought, then I should concentrate on the 20 percent that generates more for me and do more of that.

When thinking critically about my past, I don't regret a moment of the time I spent adding interesting content to my blogs. The learning curve I went through will always be an important part of what made me a successful blogger.

After blogging for a few years, I realized that I want to make an even bigger impact in people's lives and take my writing skills to the next level. So, I put all my journals together, added with my experience and write an entire book teaching others how to create a successful blog.

If you're thinking about starting your own blog, this book should be helpful to you. If you already have a blog, that is fine. I'm sure you will take some ideas from it to help direct your efforts and achieve a level that might not have been attainable before.

One of the biggest secrets I can share about blogging, one that I quickly came to understand from other successful communicators, is that you have to be passionate about what you're writing.

Past successful bloggers realized they needed a platform to showcase their ideas, and once they got going, their blogs built a loyal following. These followers mostly remain loyal and follow bloggers through their careers when move into authoring or public speaking.

But where does one begin with creating a platform? One that can fight its way through the noise of Internet traffic? Is it even possible in our fast-paced world to accomplish this magnificent feat of ingenuity? Is the "golden age" of blogging over? Is writing a blog even worth the effort?

Well, the age of blogging is far from over and people will always embark on this task from now until infinity. A passionate and creative blogger will be found, and you must attempt to do so if you want to spread your word.

But what if I don't have a message? I hear you say. Well, what are you passionate about? There's always somebody interested in your passion. Tell that to the world.

This book has been written to teach, coach, inspire, and help you to grow your platform and spread your word beyond the stratosphere of success. It doesn't matter if you have just begun this task or have been at it for ages.

I have tried my best to focus on the practical things you can do to achieve this goal and laid out each step as best I can to help you plan and implement a strategy that builds you a lifetime audience.

The tools I will teach you should help you reach your blogging goals. Goals like creating a blog, making more money, building a passionate and supportive audience and nurturing a platform that you can leverage to achieve even greater success with your future pursuits.

When I learned that I could make money doing what I loved, it seemed so strange. It seemed completely unnatural, and I fully converted from being an absolute skeptic as I watched the advertising revenues roll in. This was the point at which I truly became a blogging believer.

From that point forward, I made it my life's mission to learn and apply everything I could about internet marketing, blogging and copywriting to enhance my skills as a professional blogger.

Now, this journey is not for the faint of heart. One of the biggest parts of starting out is knowing yourself and knowing what you are passionate about.

Once you have that, I can help you transform that passion into a successful platform that you can use to achieve your ambition.

I'll be giving you an insane amount of advice and an incredible number of actions for your to-do list that may feel overwhelming but this is a process, and to really improve takes time.

Remember, we need not rush for greatness, but should try to keep making progress at a good pace. Procrastination isn't our friend.

But allow me to be clear: We will not compare ourselves to others on this journey. Only compare our past efforts to our current efforts and our past abilities to our current ones. There is no room for discouragement or self-pity, only self-accomplishment and empowerment.

One more piece of vital advice: If your primary goal in starting a blog is only to make money, your chances of success are very slim. Readers can tell passionate writers, readers can dissect the genuine from the fake. Be the genuine article, write about something you are passionate about, I can't stress that enough, its why I put the word passion in the title.

I've looked at it and tried it from every angle. I've learned that there is only one accurate way to maximize the potential profit, and that means writing. Thoughtful, interesting, practical content that keeps readers on the edge waiting for more is your very best way to make a success of your blog.

To really get traction and see success compound

your blog must provide actual value. Focus your efforts around giving rather than taking and on being helpful and sincere. Just be yourself, the best version of yourself.

Blogging is only one to make a living. There are a lot of easier ways to make money out there if that is your number one goal. So, at first, I would say that at first it's much better to think of your blog as a side hustle.

As it grows and becomes more established and profitable, look towards expanding it further. It may quickly become your greatest income source. But if you are only looking for profits, it may not be the best opportunity out there.

What I'm trying to say is that it is much better to look holistically at your blog and see it as a center-piece to an even greater movement. Think big and make your blog fit into that bigger picture.

An Introduction to Blogging (Chapter 1) - Action Items

. . .

1. Think about what you are passionate about, write a list of broad hobbies and interests.

2. Think bigger than just a blog. What sort of movement could be started from your passion?

3. Consider starting a new blog if you don't feel passionate about what you've already started.

CHAPTER 2: SETTING UP YOUR BLOG

So you're ready to create a blog. When embarking on such an effort, the first thing you should consider is what you are passionate about. There is a famous saying 'go with what you know,' and if you do that, you're starting on a winning track.

I would recommend spending some serious time thinking about this. Generally, you will be much more successful in your efforts if you pick a subject that you are seriously interested in.

Think about it: Why not research more what you know and become a master in that field, while on your journey to financial independence? Let me expand on this more to see if I can help you refine your focus, assuming you don't already have your heart set on a passion or interest for your blog.

It can be difficult settling on a focus or primary topic for a business or blog. Some of these steps might be useful in helping you determine what that might be:

1. First ask yourself above all what are you most passionate about?

2. Then ask yourself is that passion something broad enough that you could devote your time and energy to writing about it and sharing it with the world. If not, return to step one and try again.

3. Next ask yourself if this is something you have a deep interest in learning more about and becoming an expert in it.

4. Do you feel you could offer content in this area that is both unique and interesting?

. . .

5. FINALLY, ASK YOURSELF IF YOU SEE A SIZEABLE GROUP OF PEOPLE OUT THERE IN THE WORLD THAT HAVE THIS SAME PASSION AND WOULD THEY BE ABLE TO CONNECT WITH YOUR IDEAS?

I WOULD RECOMMEND THINKING of a principal theme or topic that is very broad, covering a lot of related subtopics, with a list of say 10 subtopics which can be further subdivided into specific categories.

HERE IS AN EXAMPLE:

TOPIC: *The Ultimate Vegan Lifestyle*

SUBTOPICS: *Vegan Food, Cooking, Personal Care, Cleaning, Travel etc.*

CATEGORIES: *Recipes, Online Grocers, Restaurants etc. (For Vegan Food)*

AFTER YOU'VE DECIDED on your topic, it's time to bring

this new blog into existence. The next step will be to determine where you would like to host your blog.

Many people set up a website as a permanent home for their blog. If this is your aim and you're intent on making your blog work at whatever the cost, I would say setting up your own website is the best way forward.

HERE ARE a few things I wish I knew when I was starting out:

*1.)	If you want your own website or a website that acts as a blog, you will first need to buy the domain name. The companies I recommend for this include Godaddy and Namecheap. Prices vary, but you can usually buy a domain name for under $10 a year..*

*2.)	You'll also need a computer server or a hosting service to connect your domain name to. Godaddy and Namecheap both offer affordably priced hosting but I prefer a company called Hostinger which is both professional and offers amazing discounts on shared hosting* *packages for people who want to own and operate over one website.*

3.) Once you have your domain name, connected it to your hosting service and get everything up and running, you can use the hosting service to install Wordpress software which you can use to create a wonderfully individual looking blog. It's foolproof and easy to do.

I CAN'T STRESS it enough that to have a great blog, you will need an equally impressive domain name that embodies your vision for the blog and lets readers know exactly what it is about.

Beyond that, you will have a major advantage if it is a .com that aligns with your site name rather than a .net or an uncommon type of address. Suitable names are short, easy to spell and even easier to remember.

I would recommend not wasting time using a 3rd party provider to host your blog, websites like blogspot.com or wordpress.com offer free blogs and a web address but I wouldn't recommend them. You'll find that your blog quickly outgrows that venue and will need to change to your own website and infrastructure once you start to grow.

So, take my advice, and once you've installed Wordpress (from Wordpress.org and not Word-press.com), the next step will be to adjust your themes and layout and start building content.

However, don't spend too much time on the design aspect of your blog at first. The key to any killer blog is interesting content, and this is exactly what you'll learn from this book.

Setting Up Your Blog (Chapter 2) - Action Items

1. Identify your primary focus, sub-topics and categories.

2. Find a name that embodies what your blog will be about and make sure that the .com domain is available for this name.

3. Purchase a domain name on Namecheap or GoDaddy and web hosting with Hostinger.

.   .   .

4. Set up your website in your hosting control panel, install Wordpress and point your domain name to your hosting provider on the site you bought your domain from.

5. Create a collection of articles and valuable content which can support a 3-6 month publishing campaign.

6. Hire a professional designer or learn how to design to make your blog look appealing.

CHAPTER 3 : THE BASICS OF WRITING A BLOG POST

One of the most important aspects of your blog should be authenticity. Your articles must highlight that authenticity and sincerity, and we must write the content for the reader.

Think of yourself as invading their time, and you want to make it up to them. You have their attention, write for them and make it worth their time. Choose your words carefully and make your content valuable.

As ADVERTISED in this book's title, the following are some very important things to keep in mind with blogging.

. . .

Good Ideas for Blog Posts:

• An interesting idea explained in as much detail as possible

• A topic that sparks a discussion

• A topic that pulls on heart strings

• A topic that gets people to open up and share

• An interesting argument that inspires people to take action

• A well-presented post focusing on quality, tone, and frequency

• A story both unique and interesting that you've seen or heard

. . .

- THE ULTIMATE RECIPE complete with pictures and a history lesson

- AN AMAZING TUTORIAL that teaches people to do something

- A SINGLE PIECE of advice or a collection of tips and tricks

- A HEART-WARMING story using words or images

- A TOUGH SITUATION you made it through and what it taught you

- AN ULTIMATUM PUSHING your reader to take action

- SOMETHING THAT MAKES your readers feel good

. . .

- IMPECCABLE GRAMMAR and spelling

- A HANDFUL of amazing photographs

- A FEW ATTRACTIVE designs and a story or commentary on each

- AN ENTERTAINING STORY with comedic elements of tension and release

- PASSIONATE AND WRITTEN with sincerity

HERE ARE some ideas and attributes that will push you further away from the profitability and true success you desire to achieve with your blog:

- LACKING passion and a focus in your writing

. . .

• PRESENTING trivial information about your life or life in general

• NEGATIVITY, a pointless rant or too many complaints

• INFERIOR QUALITY PHOTOGRAPHS

• LACK OF A NICHE or organization to your posts

• LACK of proper grammar or incorrect spelling

• DODGY SALES WRITING with dubious affiliate links

• LACK OF CONSISTENCY, posting too often or not enough

• POOR DESIGN and layout of your blog or its posts

. . .

- LACKING AUTHENTICITY, lacking an attempt at connecting with your readers

TRY to keep these points in mind as much as possible, while also being confident enough to explore outside these best practices to develop your own formula and process.

These points are meant to help you develop a better understanding of what it takes to create an epic and interesting blog that has your readers coming back for more day in and day out.

Now, getting into the nitty gritty. Let's talk about the way you handle blog posts. Different people have different styles for creating content. Many lack motivation and only post on a whim when they feel inspired to do so.

Now I'm not saying you can't be successful when doing it this way but there are a few reasons this might not be best for the blog and your efforts to really share your amazing content with the world. But, for me, consistency is key.

People are creatures of habit. They love nothing more than a good old routine. It's that routine you need to be part of, and the best way to break into that is by posting regular, fresh content.

I suggest setting up a list of article topics and titles and have a consistent publishing schedule. You should give each topic in your list a due date, or be disciplined and write an article every few days. But be consistent.

HERE'S **an example list of article topics for 'The Ultimate Vegan Lifestyle' blog I proposed in the last chapter:**

1) ALL ABOUT VEGAN FOODIES, who they are and what they love to eat.

2) ALL ABOUT VEGAN RECIPES, delicious dishes for 2019.

3) VEGAN FASHION IN 2019.

4) VEGAN SOCIETY and culture to fit in with the crowd!

. . .

6) THE ONLY interview with a vegan you must read in 2019.

7) NUTRITIONAL ADVICE from a true vegan.

8) VEGANISM and fitness go hand in hand, an integrated approach.

9) 20 INTERESTING facts about being a vegan.

10) GLOBAL TRAVEL destinations for a true vegan.

I HOPE this list of topics gets your creative juices flowing. Organization will pay off massively. And as your blog gains momentum, it's important to have a plan. At this point I've been giving advising you under one basic and important assumption that you love writing.

If what I've explained above intimidates you, that is fine. Every recent venture can seem intimidating at first, but as your skills strengthen the intimidation will evaporate as you become a professional blogger.

It will require hard work and dedication and if you don't consider yourself to be the most creative of writers, that is also fine. Practice. Write as often as you can and your writing skills will quickly pick up pace. .

Over the past few years the media has propagated a fallacy about the level of commitment it takes to become an outstanding writer. In 1990 Anders Ericsson completed a study which resulted in some obvious conclusions. He found that if someone wanted to become an expert at something, he should practice it for at least 10,000 hours.

That means practicing forty hours per week non-stop for five years. If you have a basic ability to share your thoughts through your writing, you're already halfway there. If you are passionate about what you write then those five years to becoming an expert in writing is almost up.

The only hour that matters is the hour you're actively working and improving yourself. Don't be intimidated, dive in with good intentions and your skill will naturally improve.

The Basics of Writing a Blog Post (Chapter 3) – Main Points

1. Be authentic and sincere in your writing.

2. Choose words carefully and find ways to add value to your content.

3. Consider planning your content out several months in advance and creating a content schedule that keeps you on track and consistent.

4. It doesn't take 10,000 hours to become an expert but it will take a high level of mindfulness and a concentrated effort to constantly improve your writing technique and content generation abilities.

CHAPTER 4 : WRITING EPIC BLOG POSTS THAT GET TRAFFIC

*a*n excellent blog post starts with a prominent topic. Look back at the list in the last chapter, I clearly defined that each article topic had a limited scope and had the potential to really engage a reader.

Now the key to taking this article idea and really bring it to life involves some clever brainstorming.

The article ideas themselves involved brainstorming, but when we're really getting down to it and focusing on a single article, it requires further expansion as we map out the journey. As the saying goes: a wonderful story requires a beginning middle and end.

Think about what your key message will be. That will become a thesis statement you will use to introduce your article and support in the body. Now you don't need a thesis statement for every article you write, but if you do, it will make things a lot easier to put an article together masterfully.

I usually like to use the 'rule of three' in articles. Basically, your main body will include three sections, which will allow for a fairly lengthy article while not overwhelming or boring the reader. Give this a shot and brainstorm a thesis statement, three sub-topics or sections in the article and a conclusion.

How you go about brainstorming is completely up to you. Some people like to use sticky notes, others a notepad, and then there are those that prefer doing everything in a word doc. This approach can make things easier and limit the amount of transcription required when you're ready to go through the process of a final writeup.

Let me take a minute to talk about some things to keep in mind as you attempt to write up your first epic blog post.

Make sure your article:

1.) **Teaches the reader something of value.**

Not all posts and articles are made equal. Have you ever come across an article that was way too long but really seemed to say nothing of relevance or usefulness? An excellent post should offer something in the way of a memorable experience and always keep in mind the fact that it should contain content of true value.

2.) Puts a unique and interesting spin on things.

It's easy to write a boring article, but it's much harder to take a topic that could be boring and spice it up a bit!

Think of adding a brief story or a joke, or something odd and out of the ordinary. This will take the article out of the mundane and into a place of excitement, drawing your reader in and making them fascinated to learn more.

3.) Is clear, concise and focused in its nature.

Earlier on in this book I referred to a thesis statement (your key point). This point should be made early on, and the body should support this idea and prove its validity. Stay on topic, work through writing up the key points in the article and make sure the content matches what you've set out to do.

4.) **Has outstanding graphics and imagery.**

It would be a mistake to avoid the use of images to support the content that you present in an article or blog post. Remember the saying a picture is worth 1000 words? It's so true.

Use pictures to enhance your content and use the right ones. A picture that illustrates a point you make or greater connects the reader to what you are trying to get across can do a lot to enhance the reading experience.

You'll need a cover image and thumbnail for the article at a bare minimum but do be sure to add more images in your content if they help bring the story to life.

5.) **Contains action items or motivates the reader in some way.**

Writing is a tough skill to master and most

professional writers struggle to really get their messaging across in the way they intend. I've heard a saying, speak to them, not at them. This advice is very relevant for the point I'm trying to make here.

If your article is based around educating the reader on a certain topic, the reader should feel like they've learned something. Afterwards, they should be motivated to learn more about the topic and excited to read more of your content too.

Now that we've covered some key characteristics of an epic blog post, it's a wonderful time to look at the subject from a profit perspective. To really see results and start earning money from your blog, you must build a huge and loyal fanbase.

But what hope does a new blogger just starting out have in doing that? Well, to grow your fanbase you'll need lots of natural search engine traffic.

If you want to get Google, Bing and Yahoo interested in ranking your articles at the front of the pack, there are a few concepts you must become familiar with.

Concepts like page rank or the way search engine results are put in order are important to understand.

Everyone wants readers to follow their blog, read

their content and become a part of their community. So, you'll have to make your articles and blog extra special, and discover how to make them more Search Engine Optimization (SEO).

So that being said, let's talk about factors that Google and other search engines find useful in determining what makes a good SEO and ensures you'll rank highly with search engine algorithms.

The following variables are vital in determining your page rank:

1.) Article Content

Foremost, focus on creating top quality content for your blog. This content should be unique and helpful to your target audience. Content that isn't unique will get you nowhere, as Google is adept at recognizing duplicate articles.

In fact, if you were to copy someone else's work word-for-word or even just steal their ideas and replicate them exactly, chances are you would be in trouble for copyright infringement.

2.) Article Length

Google and other search engines place more value on longer articles. It is important to elaborate on a subject if you want authority. If your article is longer than your competitors in the same arena, you will become the authority figure for that subject.

Remember, there are algorithms at work here behind the scenes unknown to the general population. If we knew the exact formula, we would most likely be millionaires, right?

Regardless, you will want to make your posts and articles at least 400-500 words each if you are counting on them to increase your page rank. This is because Google tracks how long each user goes to a certain page, and assumes the article must be good if the visitor sticks around.

3.) Keywords

THIS IS important for SEO and increasing your Page Rank.

It's a splendid idea to use your target keywords several times in an article.

Don't go overboard with the keywords, however, or Google may mark the particular article as spam.

If you use your keyword three to four times in any given article, you will be on the right track to gain momentum in this arena.

4.) Volume

IF YOU ONLY HAVE A FEW articles/posts, chances are they will not consider you as noteworthy as a blog with an enormous quantity of valuable articles similar to your own.

So you need to write as much quality stuff as often as possible, which will help your website get indexed by Google.

Keep in mind that after your page is indexed, Google and other search engines have bots that crawl through your content regularly looking for updates and recent posts.

The more content you can provide your readers with, the better your chances of getting listed as a site of importance. Also, it's inevitable that your published content uses your keywords in higher volume, which is a real consideration in page rank.

5.) Backlinks

.   .   .

A BACKLINK IS a link that connects a forum, directory, website or blog back to your page. In regard to page rank this is the bread and butter of the trade.

Without prime quality backlinks you will struggle to get your page listed for relevant keywords on page one or two of Google. Without them your content will be buried in the search engine's vast list of indexed pages.

Although backlinks are very time consuming to create, it should be your goal to spend a significant amount of time getting featured articles on other well-known blogs and making sure they link back to your own content relevantly.

Don't forget that the links you create should also apply to what you write about. If your subject is the Amazon rainforest, it's no good posting a ton of backlinks on blogs and forums talking about skydiving.

6.) Age of Content

Search engines are complex creatures made up of instructions called algorithms. There are rules a search engine uses to decide what value to place on your content and where to put you in its ranking system.

The age of your content plays a role in this decision as older and more established content gets credit for being around for so long and for generating and maintaining consistent interest.

I recommend that you really spend some time going over your content based on these factors.

If you work towards following the criteria set out above, your epic posts will be tuned and ready to reap the benefits they deserve from the electronic spiders exploring the vast network we refer to as the worldwide web.

The credibility of your site and its content and the page rank associated with it will come in time. The older your blog gets, the more credibility it will receive, as long as your content stays fresh.

The most famous blogs with the largest readerships don't have just one epic blog post or article in their catalog. They have an entire collection.

The key to success is consistency and the combination of both quality and quantity. The two together can become a powerful force for growth.

Each epic blog post that you add will supercharge your fanbase and bring loads of natural traffic from Google.

It will also become indexed with a high ranking for other search terms which will help draw in new visitors.

Writing Epic Blog Posts (Chapter 4) – Main Points

1. Follow the rule of 3.

2. Brainstorming extensively often results in epic blog posts.

3. Make your blog posts useful, interesting, clear and concise.

4. Don't be afraid to spend time making your content visually appealing with unique designs that support and enhance the content.

CHAPTER 5 : USING DESIGN ELEMENTS IN YOUR POSTS

*I*f I had to decide between written content or graphical content as to which is more important, without a doubt, written content will always be the cornerstone of your blog.

But there is a catch, one I would like to explain right now. To get people to actually read your content, you have to catch their eye.

Without proper application of graphic design as it relates to your website and blog posts, you won't be able to catch the eye of readers who have increasingly higher expectations for online media.

The truth of the matter is that it doesn't matter how good your content is. You must have amazing graphic design elements to engage your audience.

Now what exactly goes into a visually appealing blog?

An attractive blog should have a design that is highly organized, simple to navigate and easy on the eyes. This means limiting the colors and patterns used and leaving a lot of white space.

Now sometimes it is hard to look at your blog critically when it comes to its design and how it is perceived by others.

It is often good to bring a few friends in as consultants to look at your blog critically and ask a few of the harder questions that need to be asked to make sure your blog can compete in this arena:

1.)   Is the design of your blog appealing and does it peak interest in the people it was intended for? Is it simple enough to navigate and clean enough to keep the attention of readers without confusing them and overloading them with colors and patterns?

2.)   Is your best and most relevant content displayed front and center?

. . .

3.)   Is it easy to navigate your website and find exactly what people are looking for? Are there recommendations to other related articles on a blog post and are they easily accessible?

4.)   Is it easy to understand what your blog is about if you were a complete stranger that had just stumbled upon it for the first time?

5.)   Can your readers quickly identify your major post categories and know how to find them? Are all fonts easily readable?

6.)   Do you have a call to action on your home page that funnels readers into an interesting article or topic? Can readers easily understand why they are at your blog and what they should do immediately after arriving?

7.)   Are the graphical elements on your homepage and articles hi-resolution and vibrant? Do they draw a person in and make them feel excited to examine the content further by clicking on a link?

. . .

THERE IS a wealth of evidence out there that all points to the same key fact, the blogs with the most simplified and clean designs become more popular and gain more traffic than their cluttered counterparts.

Think about your own blog design and try to focus on the bare minimum.

Focus on limiting what is presented to only what is needed by people and go through your website as if you were a stranger to ask yourself the following questions?

Do I feel comfortable with the layout? Can I find the article I was looking for easily? Does this look like a professional blog?

There is definitely room to apply creativity and your own personal style in your blog, but just limit it a bit and think about your audience and how they will react to it.

Remember that designs alone won't make your blog successful, you'll need amazing content to keep your readers coming back. But they may never dig deeper without a nice eye-catching design to lure them along until your words win their heart!

Now here are a few famous blogs that really win

the hearts and minds of their audiences through the magnificent combination of prime quality content and eye-catching design.

1.) Mashable

The first thing that really stands out to me is their header image. Riveting, though provoking and slightly unusual, this header really draws visitors in deeper.

Then you've got the bold colors, the wiring over-lay, the gripping pupil and the contrasting text.

Now, regarding the layout, you can see that Mashable breaks its content into three noticeable sections on the homepage.

Notice that they list recent posts on the left in the smallest-sized thumbnails. This is a superb strategy as most people when returning to a site or even visiting for the first time are more likely to scan a page from left to right as that's the way we have programmed our brains to take in English content.

Then you have the "What's Rising" posts that are displayed in the center column as large thumbnails.

Finally, you have the "What's Hot" posts that are shown to the right, also as large thumbnails.

This is a three-column approach that displays content to help offer readers that can offer readers a choice regarding the news that matters to them the most.

2.) Brit + Co

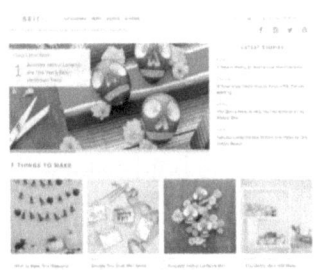

There is no disputing the fact that the Brit + Co homepage is clean, warm and welcoming.

One thing that is very impressive is how they can

present a significant number of articles while leaving it free of clutter and distraction.

The design allows content to be found easily, and the layout is logical and organized.

Another thing that was impressive was how they spiced up the blog to match the current season with avocado jack-o'-lanterns.

Very suitable for an article served to fans and loyal followers in October right?

Beyond that, they really found a colorful and fun photo to bait readers and get them interested in the story's content.

Finally, inspect the website's header and specifically the way they use it to highlight trending content.

It is a very subtle way to promote new content without being too in-you-face about it.

There are many things to admire about Brit + Co but it is also important to note that different platforms work better with specific blogs. There isn't a one size fits all approach to promoting.

3.) BarkPost

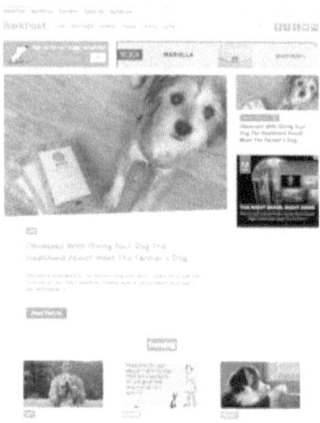

It's a known fact dogs make for great blogging! So it is only natural that a blog dedicated to life as a dog owner would be insanely popular and generate loads of interest and a huge fanbase.

BarkPost, is a fantastic example in design and layout for many reasons. Notice how they make it easy to subscribe with the call to action right above the featured content.

After looking at all these marvellous design examples, take a moment to think about your own blog and its design. Are there areas that you think you could improve upon to bring it more in line with best practices?

There isn't a single right way to design a blog or its high resolution article thumbnails and graphics but basic concepts like making an image eye-catching an thought provoking will help bring some added appeal and interest to your blog.

In the next chapter I will discuss things to think about with making posts that have the real potential to be profitable, so I hope you're ready to really kick things into overdrive!

Using Design Elements in Your Posts (Chapter 5) – Main Points

1. Utilize high resolution designs to make your blog and its content more appealing.

2. Make sure fonts used match your site and aren't too boring.

3. Optimize layout to offer a simple and visually appealing way to navigate your blog.

4. Learn from some of the most popular blogs on the web and note elements you'd like to apply to your own blog.

CHAPTER 6 : SEO AND PROFIT CONSIDERATIONS

*G*reat, you're back for more, huh? Ok, let's take a moment to review an important factor in your blog's success.

Yes, I'm referring to Search Engine Optimization (SEO), something that can literally make or break your job when it comes to winning traffic and making profit with your blog.

In regard to SEO, the following are the most important factors in getting your pages ranked high in the Google search engine:

1.) Article Content
2.) Article Length
3.) Keywords

4.) Volume

5.) Backlinks

6.) Age of Content

Alright, now on to the good stuff. I assume by now you have created a blog and tried your best to optimize it for a search. Hopefully, you have also created a few "anchor articles" i.e. lengthy articles with in-depth analysis of your subject.

If it's our goal to generate natural Google search traffic, we will need to make our site more important than sites which are above us in the search results.

Google looks at each "backlink" and shares merit and strength between your page the one you linked to. So it is logical to assume that we need to place links on sites that have a higher page rank and have a subject relevant to ours.

The following are places you may want to place content and backlinks to improve your SEO:

1.) FORUMS AND GUESTBOOKS
These sites won't get you too much of a boost, but they definitely will not hurt. Make sure the forum or guestbook

is on a site with higher page rank in one of your target keywords and also try your best not to leave a spam comment.

Look at the forum and contribute something relevant. This way you will not only leave a backlink but you may also make some friends and generate some subscribers.

2.) BLOGS AND RELATED WEBSITES

Try your best to find blogs with the same keywords as your own, read their content and provide insightful feedback on the comments section of your favorite articles. You may find that most bloggers are very open and willing to help you in your quest if you approach them the right way. Encourage them to visit your site and request feedback and suggestions for improvement. Not only will you be gaining excellent backlinks but you will also create allies that may very well help to catapult you to success.

3.) SOCIAL NETWORKS

Sites like BuzzFeed, Delicious, Technorati, Digg and Zimbio are brilliant places to claim your blogs, attach your sites and create profiles. These sites have enormous amounts of traffic, and even better, its traffic that is looking for the content that you provide. Getting an excel-

lent reputation with these sites will not only increase your traffic but will also most likely assist your page rank.

4.) PUBLICATION WEBSITES

There are several sites that let you publish articles free of charge. The articles are then featured in their community and sometimes they are syndicated outside the community to interested parties.

If someone publishes your work verbatim, google will find out when its bot crawls the page and your page rank will go up! This is why I previously emphasized original content so much. If it's not original, it will not help. Anyway, the key to gaining page rank from these publication websites is original content.

MY RECOMMENDATION WOULD BE to consider re-writing your favorite articles and submitting them to GoArticles.com. This way you will have your original content and you will have a re-write posted with their site.

Google will check out their page, identify the article as original content, and give your backlink credit. There you go, that's an instant boost in credibility!

. . .

HERE ARE A FEW IDEAS THAT SHOULD HELP YOU GET
INTO THE MINDSET OF MAKING YOUR BLOG POSTS
PROFITABLE:

1.) You can write a review on your blog about something that you have tried and liked. Give the affiliate link to people so they can try it too. If they follow your advice, you have helped them and yourself. Generally, I find it's best to recommend something that I like myself so I'm not left with affiliate remorse.

2.) You can write reviews about products and services that you didn't like. Not only will you be providing the rest of us with a great service, but you will create useful content that will eventually drive more traffic to your site.

3.) You can do paid reviews of products on your blog for companies like PayPerPost or Associated Content.

The fact of the matter is that there are a million ways that you can get paid for your opinions. Why not take advantage of some of them assuming the opportunities allow you maintain your authenticity.

If you're like me, you've been to a million websites and blogs with promises to make you rich if you just buy their "wonder" product or sign up to their email list for their "special report."

I will not lie, making money online with your blog is hard work!

It takes time, dedication and lot of planning and footwork. The rewards far outweigh the costs.

It will all be worth the effort when your blog is up and running and you are towards the top of the page in Google for search terms that match the content you are presenting.

You will also see the value in having a very substantial subscriber base and the passive income required to support yourself, free up your time and allow you to do what you want to do.

No longer will you be at the mercy of an employer that doesn't care about you or your well-being. Someone told me something a long time ago that has stuck with me to this day.

They said, start working towards achieving your dreams or else you will quickly find yourself working to help complete someone else's.

There are millions of online advertisers out there

and only a tenth as many online marketers, the odds are on your side, so if you want to blog about something you like and start cashing in on the lucrative opportunity to be rewarded for your efforts, follow me.

The first way and probably the best way to leverage advertising on your blog is with "Google Adsense."

This is by far the easiest service to become affiliated with if you want to place ads on your blog.

Each time someone clicks on one ad you will receive a contribution depending on how much value is placed on the particular ad.

After utilizing this service, you may also want to diversify your advertising with Affiliate partners.

Advertising with the program can become very profitable once your site has a high quantity of web traffic flowing through.

Google offers another program called Adwords, a program in which you can pay them to place links to your own site on other people's websites.

This could be a source of traffic for your blog if you invest and dedicate a budget for this activity.

I have found that the best traffic is the traffic you get for free through multiple links and high search ranking.

Be warned though, chances are you will not make a lot of money through Adsense when you first set up your blog.

It takes time and effort to build web traffic, but it is manageable.

When you hear stories of people making tons of money from setting up advertising on their blogs with Adsense, they may claim that they haven't been running their sites for long.

Keep in mind that it's possible they are lying or embellishing. They may own an entire network of multiple blogs and websites focusing on different niches, and each one may generate a paltry amount of revenue.

They wouldn't want to tell you that because it would be much less of a chip on their shoulder to brag about! But given this point made above, I'd pose the following question to you.

Do you want to make money blogging or do you just want to write about something you love?

Wrong answer. It was a trick question because if you are doing it right, the two should go hand in hand!

SEO and Profit Considerations (Chapter 6) – Main Points

. . .

1. USE PROPER SEO TECHNIQUES TO GAIN FAVOR WITH GOOGLE SEARCH

2. FIND ADVERTISING PARTNERS LIKE ADSENSE THAT YOU CAN   EFFEC-
TIVELY MONETIZE

3. BALANCE PROFIT WITH PASSION.

CHAPTER 7 : USING PINTEREST TO PROMOTE YOUR BLOG

*T*here are very few websites out there on the web today that can do as much as Pinterest can do for promoting your blog.

This is because we live in a world of sound bites. Most people don't read articles these days, they read headlines.

They don't listen to music; they watch music videos. Some people may still spend days scanning Facebook for new and interesting posts, but the numbers become more sparse every day.

However, there's a growing minority which prefer Instagram which takes a much more short and visual approach to social media.

Metrics show that Instagram is steadily becoming the leader in social media and it all can be traced back to our fast-paced soundbite driven world.

Now, with Pinterest there's a few things I'd like to point out if you are ready to kick your blog promotional efforts into overdrive.

The first point I'd like to make is that your image needs to be epic.

Not only must it be visually appealing but it must convey something interesting about your story, it must bait them into reading your article.

IN A RELATED ARTICLE **published by Curalate Insights they made a few major points on this topic:**

1.) Pins without faces are far more likely to be re-pinned.

2.) Bright images are better than dark images.

3.) Colorful images are better than monochromatic images.

. . .

4.)   Close-up shots are more likely to be re-pinned than panoramic shots.

5.)   Warm colors are more likely to be re-pinned than cool colors.

ANOTHER INTERESTING POINT that I'd like to make about Pinterest revolves around the way people use it.

The website encourages people to make a collection of images they resonate with.

This means that if the images used to promote your posts are inspiring, thought provoking or just plain weird, the chances are a lot better that people will collect the images you provide and in doing so, share your content with their own network.

The power of social media should not be over-looked and using this approach can get you some powerful results.

The tradeoff is that if your image simply inspires them but doesn't draw them into your content, you've only completed half the job.

There needs to be a powerful attraction and an urgency to dig deeper by clicking on your post and reading your article.

This can be a tough challenge to overcome but with a bit of care and effort we can certainly accomplish it.

Fortunately, Pinterest is easy to use and one of the first things you'll want to do is register for the site and create a 'blog board.'

Creating a board on Pinterest specifically for your blog articles is an absolute must.

Your board will make it easy for your followers to find your blog posts, and it will attract new users and create new followers of both your board and your website if you can ace your pins.

Now I'd like to share a few insanely popular blog board pins that have huge fan bases.

Pay close attention to the images, content and overall presentation of these pins.

ALSO TRY **to inspect the title and description to see if you can identify any useful patterns in them:**

1.)   Recipes - Collection by Joy Cho / Oh Joy

NOTICE HOW APPEALING the food looks in each recipe image. The titles are very short and clear. The descriptions start off in a positive and light-hearted way.

LET'S LOOK AT ANOTHER, **shall we?**

2.) *Maryann Rizzo – Everything.*

Maryann Rizzo is an interior designer and the second-most-popular Pinterest Influencer, with over nine million followers. Her top Pinterest board is "Everything," which has over four million followers and acts as a depository for pins she has yet to categorize.

One thing that catches my eye about all these images is the care and effort that must have gone into selecting them.

A lot of blogs place a big focus on lifestyle and knowing the target audience well allows bloggers to dial in their content to really appeal to who they are reaching out to.

Everything seems to do quite a magnificent job with that and there also seems to be a delicate balance between random related images and marketing based images like the lemon cake image that can be seen in the bottom left corner of the example above.

So just to quickly summarize what needs to be done to take full advantage of Pinterest for blog promotions, let me restate a few points.

AFTER YOU WRITE a blog post and pin it to your blog board, remember to include:

1.)   A brief summary, or quote, from the article.

2.)   A grand image that represents your post.

3.)   A link directly to your blog article.

Now, so far, I've only discussed blog boards. You'll also want to create other types of boards on your Pinterest account.

The boards you will want to create are categories designed to really connect and resonate with both your business and your market.

This can be difficult, but if you pin mixed content in boards with relevant titles, you'll be able to gain a lot of traction.

Content like products, household tips and lifestyle images that relate to your board theme, have been proven to generate enormous amounts of additional traffic and interest. Don't forget to include related links back to your blog.

In fact, these are tips that should apply to all your blog promotion pins, keeping in mind that you need to show readers how your blog article fits within the personal or emotional context of your board theme.

Keep psychology in mind as you build your pin empire. Let me give you an example of this in action:

Example:

There are few companies that really can pin better than Whole Foods, a company that really leads the way at driving traffic to their blog through Pinterest.

Currently, they have over 55 boards relating to recipes, health, beauty and family tips. Furthermore, they have boards like their "Who wants dinner?!" which are filled with pins that generate massive amounts of traffic for their recipe blog site.

Now that I've covered the basics of boards and how they can be used with your blog post pins to generate traffic, let me move on to how to maximize the effectiveness of images regarding your pins.

Pinterest lives and breathes visuals. Sometimes it can seem a bit confusing why images could be so important when your principal goal is getting users to read your content.

It seems counter-intuitive to provide brilliant images that may distract users from reading but studies have shown that amazing visuals, have been proven to entice Pinners to click through to your blog post.

Think of Pinterest as an elaborate glossy magazine full of stunning eye candy.

Ignoring the danger of sounding repetitive, to capture the attention of a reader from the site, your pins need to really catch the user's attention and get them to click on to your content.

According to Dan Zarella, a researcher and known authority with Pinterest has shown in his study that long visuals get the most 'rePins'.

So don't be afraid to go long and post infographics on the site.

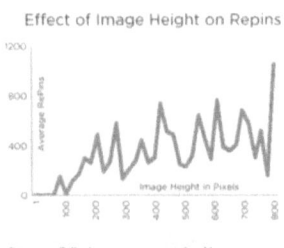

Effect of Image Height on Repins

Takeaway: Taller images are more repinnable.

Although we all wish that there was some magical way to just press a button and let Pinterest take over finding us hordes of hungry content consumers, sadly it just isn't quite that easy.

An effective social marketing campaign will require you to engage with your followers.

This is especially true if your goal is to turn Pinners into blog readers.

The more you actively engage audiences on Pinterest, the more likely it is that they will have the inclination to want to connect with you on your blog. That being said, how can that goal be accomplished?

HERE ARE IDEAS TO HELP YOU GET GOING WITH ENGAGEMENT ON PINTEREST:

1.) PIN THOUGHTFUL, ORIGINAL AND RELEVANT CONTENT.

2.) BE CONSISTENT AND PIN OFTEN SO YOUR PINS GET SEEN IN BY YOUR FOLLOWERS' IN THEIR FEEDS.

3.) DON'T FORGET TO FOLLOW BACK!

4.) CHECK OUT YOUR FOLLOWERS' BOARDS AND PINS. YOU WILL FIND CONTENT IDEAS THERE THAT APPEAL TO THEM.

.   .   .

5.) ASK QUESTIONS.

6.) REPIN, LIKE AND COMMENT ON THE PINS OF FOLLOWERS.

7.) REPIN INDUSTRY LEADERS AND OTHER APPEALING CONTENT THAT WILL CONNECT WITH YOUR OWN FOLLOWERS.

Now you are probably wondering why I've spent so long on this topic in my book.

The reason I've gone into this topic so extensively is because Pinterest has become a very mature social networking site.

It has a vibrant community of diverse readers which makes it a powerhouse for promotion.

I hope the information I've presented in this chapter is valuable in helping you really get a leg up in expanding your blog's popularity and user base.

Using Pinterest to Promote Your Blog (Chapter 7) – Main Points

. . .

1. FACEBOOK HAS BEEN LOSING GROUND TO SOCIAL NETWORKS LIKE INSTAGRAM AND PINTEREST.

2. SOCIAL NETWORKS LIKE PINTEREST PROVIDE A VALUABLE OPPORTUNITY TO BLOGGERS TO GROW THEIR FANBASE.

3. SETTING UP A BLOG BOARD ON PINTEREST SHOULD BE YOUR FIRST PRIORITY.

4. CREATING TOPIC BASED BOARDS AND POPULATING THEM WITH RELEVANT IMAGES THAT APPEAL TO YOUR TARGET MARKET SHOULD ALSO BE A PRIORITY.

5. REMEMBER TO ENGAGE WITH USERS AND REALLY TRY TO BUILD RAPPORT WITH THEM, IT WILL PAY OFF IMMENSELY AS YOU STEADILY GO ABOUT PROMOTING YOUR BLOG.

CHAPTER 8 : EMAIL LISTS, SEO AND VIRAL MARKETING

*S*omeone once told me that the only things you own on the internet are your digital products, your email list and your website. We rent everything else.

I completely agree with that statement and would argue that as a successful blogger you need to attempt to build an empire by focusing on all three.

In fact, there are many bloggers out there that remain completely focused on only growing their email lists.

This is because they recognize the true value and power of having a community of interested and loyal followers to nudge towards your new content and products.

With a solid email list, you'll have a hungry population of potential buyers ready to go through your sales funnel.

They may buy your products such as e-books, memberships in programs you've created or even physical products.

There are other bloggers who still attempt to grow their subscriber list but prefer to make a more subtle approach to sales and conversions, perhaps with an e-newsletter or regular digital publication.

The merit in this approach is that it is a very effective way to engage loyal readers and fans so that being said, an email list can really become one of the greatest income sources for your blog.

Especially if you are effective at building your base and doing targeted marketing through it. Think about it this way, if they love the content on your blog, wouldn't they also be interested in your e-book or course?

Now that I've discussed the importance of creating and building an email list, let's talk about how to go about doing that. There are several services that offer some superb tools in building your list and automating it.

Personally, I find MailChimp is fantastic if you

are just starting off. The pleasant thing about the service is that you can collect up to 2000 contacts and send automated emails to them regularly at no cost!

Lots of bloggers struggle at first in generating an income, so it's always great when you can use a service like this to add value without breaking your budget. Other services that come highly recommended include both MadMimi and Aweber.

But now that I've covered why you need a list and what service you should use to manage your list, let me talk about how to go about building your list:

1.) TO GET EMAILS, YOUR BLOG VISITORS SHOULD BE PROMPTED TO PUT THEIR EMAIL IN A SUBSCRIBER BOX. NOW THIS BOX SHOULD BE PLACED IN AN ACCESSIBLE PLACE, BUT YOU MUST EXPERIMENT WITH HOW AND WHEN THE OPPORTUNITY IS PRESENTED TO THEM. I WOULD SUGGEST RATHER THAN JUST MAKING A SINGLE ATTEMPT, LEAVE A SUBSCRIPTION BOX IN SEVERAL PLACES.

SOME PLACES I'VE FOUND EFFECTIVE FOR PLACING MY SUBSCRIPTION BOX AND GETTING SUBSCRIBERS ARE

AT THE TOP OF A WEBSITE'S SIDEBAR. IT ALSO WORKS WELL IF YOU CAN PUT IT SOMEWHERE IN YOUR HEADER OR A BAR AT THE VERY TOP OF THE WEBSITE. FINALLY, I'VE ALSO FOUND THAT A POP-UP BOX FOR EMAIL SUBSCRIPTIONS CAN BE EFFECTIVE.

2.)   NOW I CAN'T STRESS THIS NEXT POINT ENOUGH. THERE NEEDS TO BE SOME OFFERING, AN INCENTIVE OF SORTS TO GET YOUR READERS TO MAKE THE EFFORT OF SUBSCRIBING. IF YOU OFFER THEM SOMETHING OF ACTUAL VALUE, THE CHANCES ARE GREATER THAT THEY MAY TAKE THE LEAP AND GIVE YOU THEIR EMAIL.

THIS INCENTIVE COULD BE A FREE REPORT OR E-BOOK, A TRIAL MEMBERSHIP IN SOME COURSE YOU ARE OFFERING OR ANOTHER DIGITAL PRODUCT THAT YOU WOULD TYPICALLY CHARGE FOR. AFTER THE USER SUBSCRIBES, AN AUTO-RESPONDER OFFERED BY YOUR EMAIL SERVICE CAN SEND OUT THE FREEBIE UPON SIGN-UP.

3.)   PERSISTENCE IS KEY. USERS MAY NEED TO BE ASKED SEVERAL TIMES TO SUBSCRIBE. AS LONG AS YOU ARE OFFERING A SUPERB INCENTIVE, IT'S ALL RIGHT TO

SET UP YOUR WEBSITE OR BLOG IN A WAY THAT ASKS THEM TO SUBSCRIBE IN SEVERAL PLACES AND EVEN PROMPTS THEM TO TAKE ACTION WITH A POP-UP FROM TIME TO TIME!

4.) SOCIAL MEDIA CAN BE USEFUL FOR BUILDING YOUR LIST. MANY BLOGGERS CREATE AN AMAZING ARTICLE THAT CAN BE PAIRED WITH AN INCENTIVE OFFERING. THEY CAN POST THIS ON PINTEREST, LEAD-PAGES.NET, AN OPT-IN PAGE PROMOTED BY FACEBOOK AND MANY OTHER PLATFORMS.

Now that I've covered the basics of email list building, let me discuss another topic that is going to be very important when it comes to growing your blog.

A topic that I recently spoke about in Chapter 6: SEO and Profitability. Yes, you guessed it, I'm talking about SEO (Search Engine Optimization).

As previously stated, to grow your following and eventually earn an income from your blog, you must learn the best practices for having your content found through Google and other search engines.

You need search engines to index your articles and lead readers to your blog and to do that you need to show the search engines that your content is important.

The thing about Google is that SEO really doesn't apply as much as it did in the past.

Google's system has become very efficient for bringing the BEST results in search. Now there are a few ways that have worked in the past that I still believe apply and help to this day in getting Google to recognize quality content.

Now, before I go any further, I'd like to make something clear about SEO in 2020.

In the old days it was easy-to-use tricks like keyword stuffing, posting backlinks in substantial quantities and a host of other tactics to fool the robots into thinking your page deserved a higher ranking that it deserved.

In this day and age search engines are much more sophisticated and it is no longer about "tricking" Google but helping Google understand what your post is about.

Be very cautious with SEO services knocking on your door promising a glorious page 1 ranking.

If you are looking to apply best practices with SEO it is still an effective strategy to craft effective title tags, meta descriptions, and meta keywords and it's easy.

I could write a whole book on this topic alone but I'd rather leave that to someone else.

One more effective way to boost credibility in the eyes of Google and show its robots that you are an authority is to use high quality backlinks to point to your relevant articles.

A backlink is a link that connects a forum, directory, website or blog back to your page.

Generally in regard to page rank and where your content is found in search results, backlinks can play a major role in showing Google your content is both important and relevant and therefore should be placed higher in search results for the related keywords.

I have had a lot of success in the past rewriting my posts and articles and submitting them to the following free sites while linking certain terms back to the original content.

This is a guaranteed way to get a large number of high quality one-way backlinks.

These are in alphabetical order so it's up to you to figure out which sites will work the best.

Backlink Sites:

http://www.goarticles.com/
http://article-niche.com/
http://articles4content.com/
http://blogtelecast.com
http://dir.salon.com/
http://news.collectors.org/
http://superpublisher.com/
http://www.amazines.com/
http://www.articlealley.com/
http://www.article-buzz.com/
http://www.articlecentral.com
http://www.articlecity.com/
http://www.articlecube.com/
http://www.articledashboard.com/
http://www.article-directory.net
http://www.article-directory.net/
http://www.article-emporium.com
http://www.articlefever.com/
http://www.article-hangout.com/
http://www.articletogo.com/
http://www.articleworld.net/
http://www.certificate.net/wwio/
http://www.content-articles.com/
http://www.directorygold.com/
http://www.ebooksnbytes.com

http://www.ezinearticles.com/
http://www.free-articles-zone.com/
http://www.ideamarketers.com
http://www.impactarticles.com/
http://www.internethomebusinessarticles.com
http://www.isnare.com/
http://www.jogena.com/articles/articleform.htm
http://www.magportal.com/
http://www.newarticlesonline.com/
http://www.niche-article-directory.com/
http://www.site-reference.com
http://www.softwaremarketingresource.-
com/marketing-article-directory.html
http://www.stickysauce.com
http://www.submityourarticle.com/articles/
http://www.webarticles.com/

THERE'S no doubt that your page rank (the order in which google places you among your competing content providers) will explode as long as you submit numerous articles with original content and stuff them with good long tail keywords. Now let me share a few ideas on viral marketing.

It almost goes without saying that if people like what you have to say, I mean, like it, they will share it. When you have amazing content, the next step is sharing it on social media.

Platforms like Facebook, Twitter, Pinterest, Google+, Instagram, LinkedIn, StumbleUpon, Tumblr, YouTube, Reddit, SnapChat and Vine will be very useful.

There are some services that can post to many of these sites at the same time so that could be a worthy option if you plan to really go to town with this strategy.

From personal experience, I've learned that Twitter can be an outstanding way to get some of your content trending.

If the goal is to gain more followers, try to use hashtags that really catch people's attentions, this strategy will be even more successful if you also combine it with trending topics.

It is very possible to generate thousands of new followers if the bird gods shine upon you and one of your tweets goes viral.

Finally, above all social media platforms, Pinterest seems to trump them all and may be the most powerful organic marketing tool the world has ever seen.

It has become the third largest social media site trailing Facebook and Twitter and it looks likely to become the king of the hill over the next few years.

One of the biggest reasons it comes so highly recommended is that research has consistently proven that Pinterest users convert to readers.

Through clever application of email lists, SEO and viral marketing you will take your blog to a level that would be otherwise unachievable.

Mastering these three areas will help you build a community of followers that will support you as you reach even substantial achievements.

Email Lists, SEO and Viral Marketing (Chapter 8) – Main Points

1. YOUR EMAIL LIST IS A POWERFUL TOOL FOR GROWTH AND IS ONE OF THE FEW THINGS YOU WILL OWN WITH THE INTERNET.

2. GETTING EMAIL SUBSCRIBERS WILL CHALLENGE BUT CAN BE MUCH EASIER WHEN YOU OFFER POTENTIAL FANS SOMETHING OF VALUE FOR ACCESS TO THEIR EMAIL.

3. SEO IS A POWERFUL TOOL TO GAIN NATURAL SEARCH ENGINE RANK-

INGS, AND BACKLINKS CAN BE A MAGNIFICENT TOOL FOR GAINING MORE AUTHORITY IN THE EYES OF GOOGLE.

4. USING SOCIAL MEDIA SITES CAN INCREASE THE PROBABILITY OF YOUR ARTICLES GAINING VIRAL MOMENTUM. PEOPLE SHARE WHAT THEY LIKE, SO MAKE YOUR CONTENT AMAZING AND SHARE IT WITH THEM!

CHAPTER 9 : MONETIZATION

*A*re you sure you want to monetize your blog?

Many people have conflicting emotions about monetizing their blog. Some people feel that it is unethical, immoral, and greedy.

If you are one of those people, I doubt you would want to commercialize it. It's natural to have mixed feelings about monetizing your blog.

Make sure you are certain about monetizing your blog before you go down the long windy road to doing it. Success requires complete and total dedication to its purpose.

Creating an income stream from your blog or website will be challenging— make sure it's what you truly want. If your blog helps people, then you deserve to earn income from it, it's as simple as that.

One of the best ways to monetize your blog with advertising is to sign up for Google Adsense.

The process is fairly simple to sign up and assuming your website or blog uses Wordpress as its content delivery system; it is very easy to integrate. Anything we do in life we should do with ambition and motivation.

As an old co-worker named "Lou" used to say, you're in the boat or yourself out of the boat, don't sail with one foot in and one foot out.

If you plan on making money from advertising, place ads everywhere and act with boldness.

If you intend to generate income from donations, then make the link visible and articulate to your audience how important it is for them to donate to your cause.

If you're selling a product, make sure it's a damn excellent one and pitch it in a way that is win-win.

Affiliate marketing is a process in which you refer or direct potential clients sometimes described as "prospects" towards a certain product or company to earn money.

Generally, you will make some commission from your referrals.

One of the best places to set up an affiliate marketing account is with a company called Commission Junction.

They are great if your goal is to make money as a digital nomad through blogging.

I recommend that you search for the company and review their requirements for a publisher account. Another potential provider is a company called Project Payday.

Take a look at these two affiliate options and also have a look on google for other opportunities.

The potential to earn money is unlimited with affiliate marketing, it's all based on performance.

Now affiliate marketing can be an excellent source of income but it can be enhanced further if there is a specialization or a niche to your blog.

Bloggers write about something that interests them. That's what keeps fueling their fire and gives them the ability to create unique and interesting content daily. Fortunately, for some, the journey is more exciting than the destination.

But why create a niche, blog or website? Why do niche websites make money?

They deliver prime quality content, information that is valuable and useful to their readership. Many times the content provide on blogs and websites is information that cannot be found at your local library or even easily found online.

This creates scarcity which creates value. When people use google to search online for something, they know what they are looking for before they search.

If you can place yourself on the first or second page of search results for your niche, chances are you will get a lot of traffic!

Many people monetize their blogs with advertisements, i.e. Google Adsense. If they don't find exactly what they are looking for on your site, they have convenient links they can use instead of going back to search again. This all amounts to making money from your website or blog.

It is up to you but having a well-defined niche could easily propel you that much closer to success!

Monetization (Chapter 9) – Main Points

1. Use Google Adsense as a key advertising tool in your income generation efforts.

.   .   .

2. UTILIZE EFFECTIVE AFFILIATE MARKETING BUT DO IT IN A WAY IN WHICH YOU DON'T COMPROMISE YOUR INTEGRITY.

3. KEEP YOUR WEBSITE AS NICHE AS POSSIBLE TO ENSURE YOUR READERS TAKE YOU SERIOUSLY AND KEEP COMING BACK TO REFER TO YOU AS AN AUTHORITY IN YOUR SPECIALIZATION.

4. EXPLORE OTHER MONETIZATION OPTIONS LIKE SELLING PRODUCTS, EBOOKS OR SERVICES IN ADDITION TO SUBSIDIZE YOUR FREE CONTENT.

CHAPTER 10 : VALUATION AND POTENTIAL SALE

*I*f you're like me, sometimes you need to reassure yourself that you're on the right track with your website or blog.

If your goal is earning money from home, you better keep cranking out that quality content and expanding your backlink network.

GENERALLY, **the value and price of a is determined by a few factors, including a few I will mention below:**

1.)   Daily, weekly, monthly and annual revenues.

·   ·   ·

2.)   The overall demand in the niche.

3.)   The quality of content and quantity of traffic the blog attracts.

ONE OF THE most famous blogs for sale back in the day was John Cow.

Most people assumed it was a witty parody of John Chow's blog. Anyway, the owner of the John Cow make money online blog sold it for somewhere between $25,000-$50,000.

Not bad for a blog that has only been around for a couple years, right?

The funny thing about the listing was that the traffic really didn't justify the price. However, the marketing behind the site was fantastic, and the content wasn't bad either.

This is an example of how good marketing, clear and concise writing and a spoof image can pay off and really help you earn money from home.

There are really two areas of focus for conducting valuations of blogs:

.   .   .

1.) INTERNET TRAFFIC.

2.) SUBSCRIBER BASE.

PERSONALLY, I think it's much better to take the passive income approach and focus on internet traffic rather than spruce a site up just to sell it and do it again.

But that being said, it is always good to have a growth strategy and an exit plan.

If we were just going to be cold and calculating in our financial valuation of a blog, here is what the financial gurus say.

The accepted valuation method that is used to value blogs is a multiple of earnings (that is a net profit of the business is after expenses and before taxes).

How this method works is the net profit of a business is determined for the last 12 months of operations.

But this doesn't tell the entire story in fact there are some other issues that this method doesn't really seem to take into account, for example:

. . .

1.)   A BLOG'S "POTENTIAL"

OFTEN WHEN YOU are looking at sites and blogs for sale on Flippa you'll see the seller talk about the potential that it has and how it is underdeveloped.

2.)   Mistakes that you've made.

AGAIN, people often talk about errors they made in monetizing their blogs and why the buyer could increase the income significantly.

3.)   Blogs without income/traffic history.

IF YOU ARE TRYING to sell your blog with only a few months of traffic and income history, you will find that most buyers may be unwilling to part with their cash. Google updates happen so frequently, and organically monetized sites are risky.

. . .

IF YOU CAN DETERMINE how much your blog is worth and ultimately sell, then there are some best practices you should consider. Thinking back, if someone had told me about all this before I sold a few of my blogs in the past, I would have really been grateful.

HAVE some restrictions on future use:

ONE REASON I don't like to disclose which blogs I've sold (other than the privacy agreements) is because the new owners have taken the blogs in a direction that really upsets me. If you sell, find out if the buyer is happy to agree to not do X, Y and Z.

HAVE THE NEXT MOVE PLANNED:

DON'T MOVE on unless you already have other projects ticking over. Now I'm not talking about things at the idea stage, I'm talking about blogs or websites that are already alive and cooking. The sale can wait, but you might not eat if one of those other projects doesn't eventuate quick enough.

UNDERSTAND what you'll be losing:

AS A YOUNG ADULT I was admittedly naïve and didn't realize that I'd lose all the brand ownership, all the way over the content quality, all the email subscribers, everything. Make sure you know that it's all going.

STAY ON BOARD:

IF IT'S POSSIBLE, you might want to ask if you can stay on board for six or 12 months as a writer or contact to make sure they take the blog in a direction that you are happy with. This leads me into my next point.

MAKE sure you'll be able to cope with losing your readers:

. . .

YOU'LL FIND that having a blog for many years can easily result in a huge following of readers, they often provide support, laughs and practical knowledge – it's hard to imagine letting that go. You might know what your blog is worth financially, but can you put a price on those friendships and relationships?

VALUATION and Potential Sale (Chapter 10) – Main Points

1. VALUATIONS CAN BE CONSIDERED ON A NUMBER OF VARIABLES INCLUDING INTERNET TRAFFIC, PAST EARNINGS AND THE SUBSCRIBER BASE.

2. DON'T FORGET TO VALUE THE BLOG'S POTENTIAL AND MISTAKES THAT HAVE BEEN MADE THAT CAN BE EASILY FIXED. THESE THINGS CAN BOOST YOUR POTENTIAL VALUATION.

3. DON'T FORGET TO SET RESTRICTIONS ON FUTURE USE IF YOU DO DECIDE TO SELL YOUR BLOG.

CHAPTER 11 : PUTTING IT ALL TOGETHER

*I*n this chapter I will just quickly review some chief points made throughout this book.

BEFORE STARTING out on this effort to create a new and exciting blog project:

§ Think about what you are passionate about, write a list of broad hobbies and interests.

§ Think bigger than just a blog, what sort of movement could you start from your passion?

§ Consider starting a new blog if you don't feel passionate about what you've already started.

When you are setting up your blog:

§ Identify your primary focus, sub-topics and categories.

§ Find a name that embodies what your blog will be about and make sure that the .com domain is available for this name.

§ Purchase a domain name on Namecheap or GoDaddy and web hosting with Hostinger.

§ Set up your website in your hosting control panel, install Wordpress and point your domain name to your hosting provider on the site you bought your domain from.

§ Create a collection of articles and valuable content which can support a 3-6 month publishing campaign.

§ Hire a professional designer or learn how to design to make your blog look appealing.

When you write your blog posts:

§ Be authentic and sincere in your writing.

§ Choose words carefully and add value to your content.

§ Consider planning your content out several months in advance and creating a content schedule that keeps you on track and consistent.

§ Follow the rule of 3.

§ Use brainstorming to increase the chance of

creating epic blog posts.

§ Make your blog posts useful, interesting, clear and concise.

§ Don't be afraid to make your content visually appealing with unique designs that support and enhance the content.

IT DOESN'T TAKE 10,000 hours to become an expert but it will take a top level of mindfulness and a concentrated effort to constantly improve your writing technique and content generation abilities.

WHEN DESIGNING **elements in your blog and the visual appeal of it, these considerations should be made:**

§ Use high resolution designs to make your blog and its content more appealing.

§ Make sure fonts used to match your site and aren't too boring.

§ Optimize layout to offer a simple and visually appealing way to navigate your blog.

§ Learn from some of the most popular blogs on the web and note elements you'd like to apply to your own blog.

Promoting and advertising your blog can be hard work, here are a few tips to consider as you try to get your blog in front of as many people as possible:

§ Facebook has been losing ground to social networks like Instagram and Pinterest.

§ Social networks like Pinterest provide a valuable opportunity to bloggers to grow their fanbase.

§ Setting up a blog board on Pinterest should be your priority.

§ Creating topic based boards and populating them with relevant images that appeal to your target market should also be a priority.

§ Remember to engage with users and really try to build rapport with them, it will pay off immensely as you steadily go about promoting your blog.

§ Your email list is a powerful tool for growth and is one of the few things you will own when it comes to the internet.

§ Getting email subscribers will challenge but can be much easier when you offer potential fans something of value in exchange for access to their email.

§ SEO is a powerful tool to gain natural search engine rankings, and backlinks can be a magnificent tool for gaining more authority in the eyes of Google.

§ Using social media sites can increase the probability of your articles gaining viral momentum. People share what they like, so make your content amazing and share it with them!

IF YOU FOLLOW the points laid out above and use them as a guide in making your blog, you will be miles ahead of where I began when I started.

In fact, if I could have benefited from this guide before I started, there is no telling where my blogs and I would be now.

CHAPTER 12: SAVING THE BEST FOR LAST

I recognize how much emphasis I put on making money with your blog in this book.

There is some truth because to become a successful digital nomad, generate income by leveraging the internet and digital communication.

However, the fact of the matter is that many of us want to become a digital nomad to get away from our computers and experience the actual world.

Money is important, but it shouldn't be our only priority in life.

Sometimes I've found that stepping away from everything is the best approach to growing my online business.

I recently took a month off and focused on quality, the more important aspects of life, expanding my horizons, trying new things, traveling and trying to focus on self-improvement.

Novel experiences can offer the mind space to generate the next grand idea.

Working as a digital nomad can easily be a full-time job for many, but it is a part-time job for many others. Many people

I've discussed this topic with have said it's impossible to make a full-time income online and doing it from blogging alone was preposterous!

But I would disagree with them all! I know for a fact that it's possible and with the right approach, discipline and dedication, you will get where you want to go.

And for those that disagree and say that they've tried it already and have gotten nowhere with it, I would insist that they try harder and at bare minimum give it another shot before throwing in the towel.

If we are talking about pure profits generated, the most successful blog I have ever launched was a blog called 'Your Blog Is Money.'

At its peak it was frequently on the first page of Google for "How to Make Money Online," a search term with over 700 million competing pages. It also ranked for several other search terms that generated a lot of traffic and income.

The website was a great tutorial source for people beginning on their road to being an internet marketer specifically for those who want to be successful with blog advertising and income generation leveraging advertisers like Google AdSense.

I would stress that if you are ready to start your own blog now, be creative, venture out into an area that you are passionate about, make it a hobby and less of a business and you'll see it take off.

But, there is one last thing and in fact, I've saved the best for last. Here's a little-known secret that I'd like to share with you.

The secret is simple and you may have already come across it without knowing or recognizing it.

If you want the best way to really find success in everything that you do, especially blogging, it is imperative that you make it your main priority to help others. Now when I say help others, I mean really help people!

If you give it everything you've got and put your heart into your work, there is a statistically proven, much higher probability that people WILL help you.

Beyond that, in an unexplained and sort of mystical way, you'll be helping yourself too!

To lay out this formula in its most simplistic form, do more of the good, less of the bad, rinse and repeat and focus on helping others.

The money will be there when you need it. Here's to your success as a blogger, someone that has now learned the secret of turning passion into profits!

David Grete was born on Jan 12th, 1985 in Seattle, WA USA. He holds a B.A. in Business Administration from Western Washington University a PGCEi (Post Graduate Certificate of Education) from Nottingham University, UK. His passion for creating world class non-fiction titles is easily found in his publications. He approaches this passion with a true desire to help others realize their dreams and become better versions of themselves. His abiding advice for those that choose to follow in his footsteps is simply that: 'you become what you think.'

ADVISE AUTHOR PUBLISHING

Thanks for reading "A Rebel Was Born On Horus" by Adric Laser!

Please take a moment to look over some of the other amazing titles by Advise Author Publishing now available in the Amazon Kindle store.

1.) The Snake That Ate Its Own Tail: A Short Story From Dystopity by Adric Laser

2.) Cooking for Kids: A Healthy Vegan Cookbook With 25 Recipes Kids Love by Serena Day

3.) Time Management Tactics: The Ultimate Guide

to Managing Your Time More Effectively by David Grete

4.) Bitcoin Basics: A Beginner's Guide to Bitcoin and Blockchain by Marc Gordon

5.) Seven Stages: The Beginner's Guide to Dementia by Doug Francis

A Few More Featured Titles by Advise Author Publishing:

1.) The Beginner's Guide to Blogging: 25 Essential Tips For Turning Your Blogging Passion Into Profits

Have you noticed how some bloggers make six

or seven-figure incomes while others struggle to even make \$100? What if I could teach you some key skills and habits that could make your blog a true success financially?

One of the biggest secrets I can share about blogging, one that I quickly came to understand from other successful communicators, is that you have to be **passionate** about what you're writing. But this book has so much more to offer.

In this book, you'll find easy step-by-step instructions on how to:

 * Setup your very own blog.

 * Analyze and select a specific niche that is both profitable and that you are passionate about.

 * Promote and market your blog using several proven social media marketing strategies.

 * Apply basic content strategy and design elements to your blog posts to make them go viral.

 * Apply 25 essential blogging tips that can help you turn passion into profit.

While you may not get instantly rich from blogging it is something you can easily build upon in your spare time and expand into a full-fledged career path. In this book you will learn everything you need to know to get a huge advantage in blogging by standing on the shoulders of some of the most successful bloggers ever to put words on a page.

<u>For less than a cup of coffee</u>, this book will literally teach you how to turn your <u>passion into profit</u>, <u>become your own boss</u> and eventually <u>leave the day job behind</u>!

2.) She Gets It Done: How Successful Women Manage Their Time

In **She Gets It Done**™ you will learn:

✓ How to transform yourself into an extremely productive person.

✓ Tips and tricks that will show you how to work smarter, not harder.

✓ How to free up massive amounts of time by looking at the big picture and delegating tasks.

✓ How to organize your time in a more logical and efficient way, leaving more time for you.

✓ How to prioritize your most important tasks and eliminate wasted time on the things that simply don't matter much.

Do you think it's impossible to find the time to do things that make you happy? Think again because, I've done it and now I want to show you how!

There's no time to wait. The clock is ticking and we need to make the most of it. Grab a copy of this book and let me show you how to really make the most from your time!

3.) Herbal Medicine for Everyone: The Beginner's

Guide to Healing Common Illnesses with 20 Medicinal Herbs

Herbal Medicine for Everyone™ is the go to guide for alleviating common illnesses through the use of over 20 medicinal herbs.

The number of handbooks and guides covering this topic can make finding the right book extremely overwhelming.

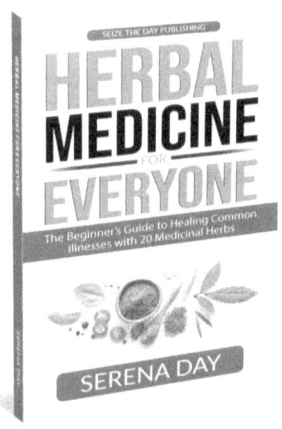

✓ Fortunately, it doesn't take a genius to begin harnessing the power of herbal medicine to cure common illnesses, it only takes some basic training and initiative.

Herbal Medicine for Everyone highlights effective herbs and homemade remedies that assist in the body's natural ability to fight off infections and ultimately cure itself of the common illnesses that plague us frequently.

This book will transform readers into junior herbalists who can easily recognize the most abundant and effective medicinal herbs that they can use to craft powerful remedies for common illnesses.

★ Included are remedies proven to be effective in reducing the severity of headaches, fevers, allergies and many other common ailments. Junior herbalists will learn the essential knowledge they need to transform into highly skilled naturopathic caregivers and gain a unique ability to apply herbal medicine effectively.

Herbal Medicine for Everyone teaches you how to use herbs as preventative and restorative medicine with:

✓ An Herbal Medicine Orientation provides the building blocks of knowledge when it comes to purchasing, making, and using herbal medicine in an effective manner.

✓ An Overview of Popular Herbs teaches you how to select the appropriate herbs for your medicinal herbal pantry.

✓ 20+ Herbal Remedies for Common Ailments with step-by-step instructions on how to make them in the comfort of your own home.

You'll learn how to alleviate stress with linden, soothe and comfort burns using marshmallow and detoxify your body using dandelion.

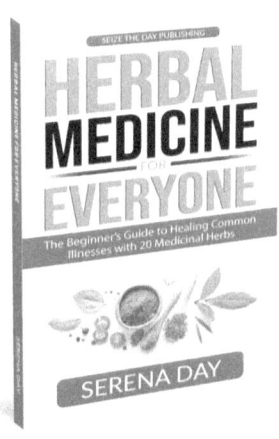

Get a copy of "Herbal Medicine for Everyone" today and ditch the store bought meds forever.

4.) Seven Stages: The Beginner's Guide to Dementia

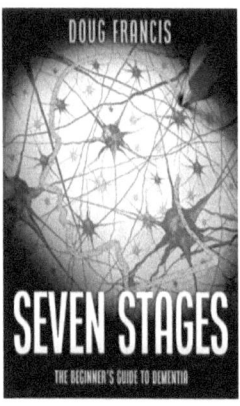

It is very hard watching a loved one suffer. When taking care of a loved one there is no doubt that the late-stage crisis that comes with dementia can be extremely hard to manage and cope with.

Although the condition strikes differently and in its own way depending on the individual, there is a real need for guidance when it comes to proper care for patients and loved ones.

It is even more important if you intend to become a caregiver to an elderly father or mother suffering from this condition. *Helping people to more confidently take care of a friend or family member during this diffi-*

cult time was what inspired me to write "Seven Stages: The Beginner's Guide to Dementia."

Statistics show that the likelihood of one suffering from dementia increases with age, and it is extremely common in those of sixty yearss of age and older. This book was written with a few important goals in mind.

In this book you will learn:

✓ *The many causes and types of dementia.*

✓ *Common symptoms and an overview of the seven stages of dementia.*

✓ *Well researched nutritional guidelines to help prepare healthy meals that can assist in mitigating the symptoms of dementia.*

✓ *Difficult end of life decisions that may need to be made for patients suffering late stage dementia.*

✓ *Taking care of someone that is in the very last stage of dementia.*

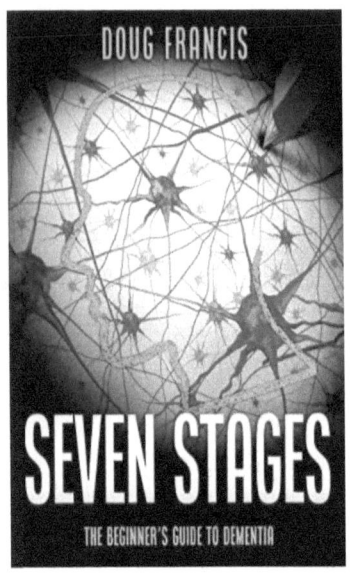